Jamie Holloway

Rosen
REAL
READERS

Rosen
Classroom™
New York

1

Robots are machines that follow instructions. Robots can help with work. Robots can also play games.

Robots start as different parts. When you put the pieces together, you build a robot.

Robots are built in all shapes and sizes. You can draw what your robot will look like. Your robot can look like anything you want.

You can make a robot taller than yourself, like this one. Tall robots can reach great heights.

Your robot can challenge other robots to play ball. Who do you think will win the game?

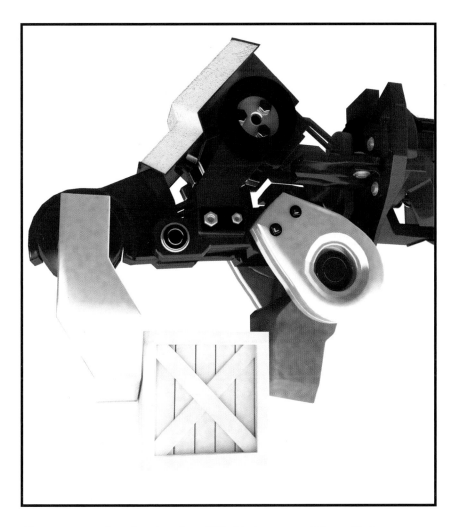

Some robots help lift things, like this one. A robot can move a heavy box.

You can make a robot a part of yourself.
This boy learns how to control his robot.
He wears special equipment that will
help him.

This girl speaks to a robot. Machines can look like people, too.

Some robots have wheels. Wheels can go fast. This girl sits on a robot with wheels.

There are many kinds of robots. What will your robot look like?

Glossary

challenge To invite into a contest or competition.

equipment Items used for an activity.

heights High places or areas.

machine A tool with moving parts that does work.